quick fire

Advance Praise for

Quick Fire

Allyson Horton's Black poems require hot water and nature fire. Her seasoned use of language is pressure cooker perfection. A blend of quick witted pop culture intuitiveness, and feminine defiant screams, this poet's work orbits into a stratosphere of excellence, while still remaining tangible enough for her audience to hold these words in their bare hands. Grounded in her community and unapologetic blackness, Horton's voice is poignant and necessary armor against the current political climate. A daughter of the grace that gave us Mari Evans, Horton's *Quick Fire* is an intentional flame of resistance against the brittle reality of American history. A powerful new voice in poetry.

—jessica Care moore, poet, activist, publisher, Moore Black Press

The most amazing thing about Horton's work is the ground it covers. After reading Horton's book, one feels as if they have traveled through the last one hundred years of Black history with a host of different characters and voices— from sharecroppers to hip-hop artists, from oracles to Bessie Smith, from homages to Paul Laurence Dunbar to Wes Montgomery. It is easy to admire the wisdom—and the music—of these poems.

—Hilene Flanzbaum
Allegra Stewart Chair of Modern Literature
Director, Writing for Wellness Project
Butler University

Allyson Horton lays bare the magic of second sight and dreams in her stunning debut *Quick Fire*. "Fact: we black women/ will come under fire through hell/ hair, or high yellow," Horton proclaims. Praise this seer singing steady and clear. Praise the lessons waiting in the lines..

—Mitchell L. H. Douglas
author of *dying in the scarecrow's arms*

quick fire

Allyson Horton

poems

THIRD WORLD PRESS FOUNDATION
Chicago

Third World Press Foundation
Publishers since 1967
Chicago

First Edition
Printed in the United States of America

22 21 20 21 20 19 18   7 6 5 4 3 2 1
Sydnee Haley, Graphic Designer: Cover Art

Library of Congress Control Number: 2017956564
ISBN 978-0-88378-403-7

To my dearest parents, sister & nieces,
with Love

In memory of Frances Mae Haley, mother of my mother, may
these poems embody in substance & soul her unrepeatable
beauty, rhythm, language & laughter.

"Granny"

May 28, 1928—April 6, 2004

Contents

Introduction

Here are poems from the root. The splayed tendrils of a black woman's life. Mississippi/Midwest bones and clay. The unbridled black woman's tongue. These poems by Allyson Horton are proof that in the age of Google and social media, the steadfastness of intricate storytelling and lyrical balance will never be lost. As Horton writes, "Truth is stranger than fruit/blacker the berry/sweeter the pluck." Horton's tongue is the rich, complicated pluck. Rapid tongue.

How is history to be written? What is buried? What revealed? Horton's voice is concise, unflinching, and balanced. She writes it down. She uncovers. She reveals. The Middle Passage, The Great Migration, Hip Hop. She renders our history from the collective and personal. These poems embrace Sankofa by looking to the ancestor past while observing the tumultuous, black present. Some of the most powerful poems are ones that pull from the specifics of Horton's life. Her lovely tome on being a young girl raised as Jehovah's Witness is thoughtful, vulnerable, and revealing. What does it mean to be on the outside of the traditions of main stream Christianity? Horton's final image in the poem of a child "handing out pamphlets. Spreading the good news" is an intelligent mixture of bittersweet longing and childhood disappointment.

Probably the strongest element to Horton's work is her unbridled love poems. Her words are sensual and brimming with desire:

> Bring your limbs to the dinner table.
> I've got bones to hack with you. Legs
> to untangle. A forked tongue to bleed dry.
> It seems the wine stained cork could not
> contain itself sitting in the middle of it all.
> What I have not sipped, I have poured
> over the boneless breast of roast chicken,
> garlic mashed potatoes and your favorite fresh sweet peas
> cold now from the autumnal draft as I pace
> back and forth gazing through the window
> at the starry-fleshed woman jutting her glowing eyes
> from afar, while the minute-hand twists
> the face on the blood-orange moon
> setting us back a thousand kisses.

Blues woman, black woman, lover woman, plain priestess of blood on the root. These poems are contemporary and classic. We find ourselves hovering above references to Flava Flav, Amy Winehouse, and a remixed Hottentot Venus then gracefully moving to Paul Laurence Dunbar and Nina Simone. Horton is a truly modern poet with a grasp of history and its relationship to contemporary issues. It is one thing for a poet to know her history, and another to relate it with dexterity and competence. She masters the tanka, the haiku, ghazals, blues, and free verse with ease. She conjures the image and masters the form.

A house, a home, a resting place. These poems offer a home where "the stretch of long road / smiles & smiles for emerald miles /where an abundance of local crops /choir crisp hymns in the rustic breeze." A black woman with a tongue raised in the "plunge & plow of tractors grinding" is writing black poems. Although rendering the landscape of the Midwest, the images also feel southern and rural and move to urban and steely. A black woman's tongue conjuring place and history, uplifting life.

Kelly Norman Ellis, PhD
Author of *Tougaloo Blues* and *Offerings of Desire,*
Associate Professor, Department Chairperson English, Foreign
Language and Literatures, Chicago State University

I.

Understanding Eve

I mean—to put it all on Satan might be a little unfair. Considering the fact that a woman has her own mind. Her own set of ribs. Her own eyes for examining both sides of a fig leaf. Nose for sensing fire in a single drop of rain. Her own lips for speaking when asked for directions. Brain for deciding left or right. A body bearing its own garden of lush fruits. And besides *His*, her own breath, coursing through each flared nostril. Own cravings scratching at the surface of her earth brown rainbow skin. Own teeth perfect for chewing the fat with a serpent. Her own seeds planted in hidden places. Her own dark voices, caprices, coiling inside. Her own solutions to curing mass ignorance, climate change, pre-inflation theories, and doubling the learning capacity of children. Her own reasons for not eating the waxed skin of an apple. And, wouldn't you say, her own ideas on how to get to the *core*.

Lot's Wife Takes the Stand

"But his wife looked back behind him, and she became a pillar of salt."
(NJKV, Genesis 19:14-17, 23-26)

i had to see
with mine own eyes
the Master at work

i had to capture
with mine own eyes
the Creator convert

spiritual king
into supreme punishment
so with an opportune twist

of the neck, i looked back
& witnessed god
become a *man*

of his tongue   destroyer
of evil doing—curator or chemist   sulphur & fire
is a father proving his point

a Maker, making it clear
flooding the speechless city
with the power of his word   imploding

the landscape with a mere *blink*
unwiring the system
with the pull of Time

lot and i lost count of the charred
corpses of women, children
blown clean out of memory

pleas of mercy were met with a plume
of ash forming searing clouds
of dust inside each nostril

my sandaled feet stood submerged
in a red pool of semen blood wine
the chalk black air reeked of remorse

still, the titanium gavel of thunder ruled
truth is—i paused in *disbelief*
the phrase 'oh my god' was coined by others before me

& as the tears streamed
down my cheeks i began to feel the sting
of what he deemed my sins.

Ghazal for a Master Storyteller

for Johnnie Mae, born April 1, 1928 Holmes County, Mississippi

To be born this way—dirt black—is to find one's feet
planted like a sharecropper. Rooted in the bitter soil
of words like slave, nigger, coon, *the Help*, sharecropper.

Red clay bloodlines will make you or forsake you. Note: the diaspora
of descendants of Ham, those who bear the burden of pigmentation
like a dark dispiriting destination: sharecropper.

Inny, minny, miney, nightstar. Follow the yellow brick sky, how far?
Up north, where we's heard niggas no longer are /chained/
to the idea of sharecropping.

In the sepia photo, I study the garments of a people unconstrained.
Hand-stitched threads marking new territory. A young couple's
countenance caught escaping the noose of sharecropping.

Reconstruction: to modernize an idea or fixed object: commission
"starving artist" to replicate unsightly sculpture. Politically correct
genuflection. Plant in urban area. Renewal of sharecroppers.

February, a month of love & remembrance—also, the coldest
shortest portion of the year. But, my migrant grandmother
has a long memory. Recollects our "share" of sharecropping.

Saturday Morning Blues

We are arks with no rooftops. Refugees
with flooded homes, levees on the verge
of breaking until a poem comes along, breathes
into our nostrils names us like Adam, curses us
like Eve. Three days is too long to be left
in the dark, so on Day Four, God created light.

We are snipped umbilical cords tied to one another.
Encased stars wailing for our Mothers. Broad stripes
& hemorrhaging hopes of one day being able to stomach
the ebb. There is a reason Coltrane wrote *A Love Supreme*.
In the end, who will love us as the planet has tried?

We have a postcard scenic history with ropes
in this country. Slip knots in a nation of red, white
& incurably blue people. Our dreams do not define us,
our nightmares knock on doors like Jehovah's Witnesses
on Saturday morning, like Mormon missionaries
who just hid their bicycles on the side of the house
attempting to sell us rainbows after the storm.

Shedding Skin

i.

I dread the rocky terrain ahead: the cumbersome season
of new-found space and lost time. The icicle moon
hanging just around the corner. The annual invitation
to spiced eggnog and corn pudding my sister will not extend.
The olive branch I will grind into a fine powder. Then smoke.
The ulcerous lesion we will plant inside our mother
whose role will be to civilize her warring daughters
through her bosom and her bible.

ii.

But, we are not god-fearing women who have learned
the restraint of Job. We are women, like Eve, who give birth,
sprout seeds, wriggle our way around the garden accompanied
by a serpent, the one with the luxurious lisp, the flamboyant
one with the double-headed penis, and double edged axe,
a snake skin feather fixed in his hat, passing out pamphlets
on how to get even by *shedding the skin*, top layer only,
which in most cases, has already been burned.

Blues in G Minor

I don't know where this is coming from. What's wrong with my hair? I just simply gelled it back, put some clips in it and put it in a bun. Are you kidding me? I just made history. And you're focusing on my hair?
—Gabby Douglas, *USA Today*, August 6, 2012

Fact: we black women
will come under fire through hell
hair, or high yellow.

Gabby Douglas learned
the hard way that to be black
is a balance beam—

a handstand of sorts
a backward flip to mother
earth—*land on your feet.*

Girl, you should straighten
your back, not your roots. Some folk
wish they had your *gold.*

Fact: we black women
must look over our shoulders
brush them haters off.

Moral Memory: On the Eve of State of Indiana vs. Mister

A girl child ain't safe in a family of men.
                    —"Sofia" in *The Color Purple,* Alice Walker

Exhibit A: the abstract memory of alien lands. Hands
roaming susceptible territory. West Indies. West Africa.
Didn't learn about conquistadores or enslavement

until fourth grade. By then I was able
to put idiom & alphabet
together like Nettie & Celie.

Like Sofia. Like Trail of Tears. Middle Passage
& everybody
who looked away

from the pull of flesh,
peeling off bones of pre-teen
females in the family.

Little girl stretched into grown woman.
Grown woman slowly inching
herself back into the child.

I never flinched at the pool
of my own blood—surname smeared
on the subpoena too.

Mothers, fathers, aunties,
grandmother. An entire continent
of first cousins—sentenced
by their own silence.

The quandary was never *not knowing.*

Not knowing what to do.
Not knowing where to find
the audacity to survive. The gut is compass.

                              Is always compass.

Where Are the Women

for minnie sue reynolds, frances mae haley & maxine moore waters

the formidable fierce undefeated women
the "you got one more time"
then *mean it* women   "*nigga, please*" women

the "have you *lost* your damn mind?"
"my own daddy didn't even hit *me*"
straight-back'd-crank'd-neck-clutch'd hip   *oh hell naw* women

struttin' they stuff with bittersweet
honey in their rocks & sways
toward self-determination

where are those willing to gather to hold
these types of pertinent conversations
with *other* women about former formidable   mothers & aunties
who sneezed black fire   sweat muddy waters
'cuz they ate the blues for breakfast
lunch & dinner   *still* made somethin'
out of the 'nothin'   stamped across
foreheads   walked high & sturdy

struttin' they funky stuff with cast-iron
guts & sharp shooting memories intact
dating all the way back to great-great-grandmothers

killin' time in southern kitchens
slicin' clean through to the white
meat of raw potatoes & onions   just for practice

where are the women
the fearless Harriet Tub(wo)man types
who'll hold the rifle or the razor
unflinchingly against mister's jugular
& resolve   not my mother
            not my sister
                not my daughter
            not my niece
not ne'er one of us *no more.*

Smelling the Coffee

His eyes refused to water. His heart dead
at the roots, stubborn like his father, cold
and gone now. The men in his family head
households of slow-brewed women: coffee bold
black like the cup he orders with no room
for cream or sugar to cloud sorghum sweet
memories of his mother masking gloom,
she saw the mug half-empty, incomplete
lying next to a husband dodging touches
while watching Monday night football, losing
sight of the fumbles slipped through his clutches.
But Val was not *his* mother—torn choosing
her man's sole happiness over her own.
Val was a woman of raw skin, teeth, bone.

The Mirror and Map of Memory

Some folks ain't cut out for indigenous stories.
Mississippi wears my granddaddy's name on it. His mother
soaked her calloused heels in its marshy flesh.
Salt still troubling the waters to this day.

Choctaw Indian swims downstream
with varicose veins visible in the legs
of great-granddaughters.

Her canvas is deep red clay
oiled with black mud.
Hair bone-straight. Thick as blood.

Up close I studied
the carved bones pillared beneath squashy cheek,
the pebbled necklace
rivery eyes,
flatland lips,
hilly breasts
each telling its own history.

The deep-rooted face
is both mirror and map
window and door.
I do not see me in her.
I see her in me.

The Invitation

after R. S.

Bring your limbs to the dinner table.
I've got bones to hack with you. Legs
to untangle. A forked tongue to bleed dry.
It seems the wine stained cork could not
contain itself sitting in the middle of it all.
What I have not sipped, I have poured
over the boneless breast of roast chicken,
garlic mashed potatoes & your favorite—fresh sweet peas
cold now from the indoor draft as I pace
back & forth gazing through the window
at the starry fleshed woman jutting her glowing eyes
from afar, while the minute-hand twists
the face on the blood orange moon
setting us back a thousand kisses.

To Examine the Body

Peering into this funhouse mirror, we granddaughters
become deluded by our own self-reflection.

What we see is not always what we swallow
but what we are left to chew on despite

our convex imaginations—mascara lash'd, wonder bra'd,
foundation powder'd & spandex'd to perfection.

A constellation of black moles illuminates the border
of my face. Big Mama appears in the strangest of places

like the back of my throat where the delicatessen of chitlins & oxtails
disrupts the last forkful of tofu. I grew up Jehovah's Witness

not vegetarian. Look at me now, blurring in & out, narrowing
my view. Life is much more palatable from this angle.

In the womb, we have no choice about where we land.
To watch the body become distorted is a turn on for some.

An embryonic flashback to the elasticity of muscle memory.
The outstretched hand reaches for an anchor in a myriad

of walls smudged like carnival glass. Dare we slide through
the dark corridor in search of our multiple selves: silly faced,

scared, thin, silvery, bloated, de-collagen'd, de-estrogen'd,
umbilical cordless souls. Blood-lined, laugh-lined

caricatures of our mothers' mothers knelt over cupping
our one rib, while the tender white meat of us

seems to fall right off the bones, like the way
your own skin begins to drag you back in time.

II.

Rising Forth

There is in this world no such force as the force of a person determined to rise. The human soul cannot be permanently chained.
—W. E. B. Du Bois

I am three generations, two grandparents & one post-antebellum
aspiration from being reared in the long-lettered state
where my Mississippi born father's father
had a hard time seeing himself surviving
the chokehold awaiting any man of deep
color averse to the idea of an invisible   existence.

Sharecropper, was not foreign to his lot in life.
Nor the bowing of heads, the daily mantra of *yessuh boss*
during the ritual of cotton-pickin', corn shuckin'
& constant worry of "Am I makin' babies
to do *this* for the rest of their lives?"

If only you could envision the sepia image
of my oil slick grandfather as a young man
age 24—brimmed hat tilted, keen nose, sly grin,
southern charm, physique: handsomely lean
not at all cut for such a blissless designation.

He was a psychological composite
of a pre-Bigger Thomas black man
wearing the façade of an uppity-minded
negro—typical massa grade "good hair" type
whose spit polished complexion
sparkled with potential.

The kind of black that would not rub off if it could.
The kind too aware of himself to be limited;
his inclination could only be tolerated.
Now this was Cruger, Mississippi, 1948,
in the Jim & Jane Crow of the long-lettered state
where the last thing a colored person
would dare imply is that he or she be *tolerated*.

16

Besides, there were other places
designed for scaling racial mountains
& my ambitious grandfather had heard
noises that a small town named Indianapolis
happened to be one of them—up North
                                    & *upward thinking?*

So with wife & baby Jimmie in tow,
Ed and Johnnie Mae set their sights west
of Mississippi's "Can't Be Satisfied" blues
west of Mississippi's ravenous river
of bottomed black bodies.

The young searching couple landed in the heart
of Indiana's wheat & wonder
corn & capitalism
                possibility & surprise.

Counting—seven children
& eleven grandchildren later   *still I rise.*
Blackwoman poet.
I inherit their struggle.
I reap an uprooted people's sown
seed planted in the soil
of a new black earth.

Self-Made Man: Checks & Balances

you try bein' swarthy as the moon's
shadow   illuminating tangled roots
of kinkless hair   lips thin as two
last dimes while underneath browning
nail beds lie clumps of rain-glistened earth
viridescent as the rind of a melon.

you try bein' the seed everyone
spits out   whole flesh sliced
into trans-atlantic wedges
white meat of you exposed   succulent dark fruit
made in the image of a god
who seldom smiles back

you try fixin' your mouth to ask another
man for permission to break bread, break
wind   make eye contact with jesus while
masterin' the art of lowerin' your chin
to balance the weight of sharecroppin'
for the rest of your aimless black life

you try hearin' the name *boy* replace
the one your daddy gave you
try standin' tall as the sky laid wide open
but not for you   bumpin' your head
on stained-glass ceilings positioned
just above the brow

you try stretchin' a dollar round
a can't see corner of blues to come
pinchin' nickels into dimes
dimes into quarters   tryin' hard
not to sell the one soul
cost you everything you got

you who arrived a man
of plantation flex & flight   8th grade education
vision muscular as a mule
carryin' a borrowed suitcase
full of hand-me-ups to offset everyone

an' he who dare puts you to the test
will only confound himself
for you know full well what beans
& brawn you be packin'

you try findin' a woman—schoolhouse learned, too
believed pickin' cotton was neither her calling
nor her lot   wanted a fine husband
babies with "good" hair   her own
house, clothes, patch quilt of peace
an' she be in the kitchen   steadily
stirrin' the pot pork-fatted enough
to feed a family of nine

an' she be well-versed in survival   Devil
& the ways of white folk   a bible woman
whose silence always supports your cause
whose plum lips & buttermilk hands help
dissolve the evening sun   rubbin' peppermint
salve into calloused grooves of heat lashed
skin cracked from the cold of everyday
eyes that refuse to accept your kind

an' later when she dips
them field tired feet into a pan
of lukewarm water   *lawd have mercy, there is a God*
an' let him tell it   She is
every honey-molasses-brown-sugar
baked-sweet-potato-glazed-woman
whose hips open after midnight
to swallow the stars one by one

Haiku

America will
always walk with a limp must
be her Wounded Knee

Long Way Travelin': The Making of *Roots*

aboard the trane with caution   listen
for directions but whatever you do next
do not, i repeat do not take a back seat
or you will immediately be asked to   jump off
an' remember, you gon' wanna hold on
to dat ticket   *trust me*
cause you will kick yourself later for not
askin' the conductor for an autograph
photos are out of the question
handshakes involve too much risk

i recommend you pack light
in fact, pack nothing at all
bring only your titanic appetite
for freedom   be willing
to die for what you believe in   god
didn't make no slaves   he made
flesh & marrow   hellion & hound
best know the difference he made
the chicken & egg speckled
black & yellow   red & white
       & in that order.

*   *   *   *   *

before sun there was darkness
blew an asphalt mist all around the edge
of the moon to create night
an' god got some big ol' lips
soup coolers they call 'em—b. b. king blue
on the inside   swear 'fo jesus!
legend has it—lightnin' hissed
behind the strings he strummed to make it rain
only one star   one lone star
embedded in the sky   the others
hadn't been penciled in yet.

*   *   *   *   *

well now…where was i? my apologies
for a moment there, i must've dozed off
an seem to have woke up to at least   a billion
blinking asterisks   that's when i know'd
i'd been hit over the head with somethin'
much bigger than me   most likely dragged
across the atlantic   caveman-style
swear when i opened my fool mouth
first thing i asked for was not a gourd
of cool water but a slice of sweet
potato pie & glass of cold white
milk to chase it down kindly

suddenly—pictured myself on a new home plate about to swing
from a popular tree   *thank god* for nightmares
only dreams come true an' when they took the drums
some of us learned how to beat the system
as in *boom-pap-boom-pap-boom-boom   pap-pap   boom pap*
as in somebody hand me a spoon
a jar of pomade an' a hot comb so i can   *yes, we can!*
straighten some of this shit out
as in when i look at barack obama
a colored man runnin' for office
i can see how kunta kinte's cut off
foot was meant to foreshadow   my own.

*   *   *   *   *

Birthday Poem

At a quarter-past forty,
I realize I have learned

nothing about survival only *escape*
how to take flight heading North

of everywhere I have landed
might could use a clue, a compass

or one of Harriet's ol' rifles to gun
down the yellow-eyed ghosts

blinking back a mapless death
giving me no other option

than to look fate & the other side
of tonight's full autumnal moon

directly in the eye & shoot.

Uncle Ben Redux

Uncle Ben, who first appeared in ads in 1946, is being reborn as Ben, an accomplished businessman with an opulent office, a busy schedule, an extensive travel itinerary and a penchant for sharing what the company calls his "grains of wisdom" about rice and life. A crucial aspect of his biography remains the same, though: He has no last name.
　　　—*New York Times*, March 30, 2007

So wise of them
to remove the baggage
from underneath his stirring eyes
unfetter him *then*
bow & tie him to the "self-made man"
one who has learned the art of skin
& grin to keep from rottn'.
So very wise of the man-
ufacturers of Uncle B's rice
to cook up something 21st century
for the brother—skim off the fat
from black-eyed peas & smoked ham hocks
swimmin' in post-antebellum juices.

I see—we here to stay　　even if
America remains lost at sea
in the shipwrecked bowels of Columbus
the myth of Uncle Tom & his refurbished cabin
Aunt Jemima's world-renowned recipe books
& now you can just add water
to your transatlantic-flavored flapjacks
of course　　a little syrup
'cause who wants to eat dry
American history.

Writer's Block (his poem by special request)

i got
a love poem
lodged
in the middle
of my throat
a savory love poem
but sometimes
i get choked   *on the bone*
i still need
to pick
with
you

Husband #2 (no charges for an empress)

poem fuh Bessie Smith

I got the blues in my left shoulder
I got the blues in both my feet

Said I got the blues in my left shoulder
got the blues in both my feet

Heard some huzzy tryin'
ta walk in my shoes
damn'd if she walk all over me

I got the blues in my back bone
got the blues in these good time hips

Heard he been high steppin'
down at the juke joint—said it's high time
I made a special trip

Lawd, when I saw him
clear in that corner holdin'
his liquor & his new gal

First thought come to mind:
Go upside two heads, Bessie
then exit wit a smile

I got the blues in my left shoulder
got the blues in both my feet

When the cops come a-knockin'
my poor heart look'd bruised
like *I'd* been beat

Husband #4

poem fuh Willie Mae "Big Mama" Thornton

I'm the kind o' wo'man
chase round after my man

I'm the kind o' wo'man
chase round after my man

Lookin' for my door keys
& my last piece o' change

Said I'm the kind o' wo'man
chase round after my man

Sniffin' for her scent
& every dime spent once again

I reckon this time it's the rent
maybe, a brand new mink

Now if I catch 'em drivin' round
in *my* car it'll drive me to the brink

Said I'm the kind o' wo'man—ain't
gon' play that 'nother wo'man stuff

Be the last tail
you chase, *hound dog,*
go' on call my bluff

Morning After Aubade

Kiss me good morning
serve me breakfast in bed I
want leftover you

Charlie's Horn

What now will become of me—who, today, finds no
anchor in the slipshoddiness of language. Nothing
to avert the curse of autumnal winds. Nothing
in this world to seduce or chronicle in a foreign
tongue. Nothing dancing on the rooftop. Nothing
drumming me back home. No polyrhythmic tides
washing me to shore. No grandiose flood sent
to trouble the waters, down here. No rescue
through the biblical blowhole of a large white fish.
No muse picking the locks on doors to rooms
where the keys have been missing for weeks.
A friend tells me I could turn to jazz and wait
for a cool breeze or a dizzying blast of be-bop
unleashing a manic chain reaction of eighth notes
that zing and zip through the sky like a brass
wing'd bird, up and away I'd fly but the truth
of the matter is—I'd just as soon get wine high

than risk Charlie's horn hitting the wrong vein.

Not Like Jazz

The clock read 7:Q4 if that tells you anything
about how the rest of my day has gone. Upside down
skyscrapers ain't got nothing on propeller-less
helicopters sitting on dubs in rush hour traffic
and I haven't even gotten to the bizarre stuff yet.
My boyfriend calls a quarter-after something suspect
and I hear a goat bleating in the background.
I want to ask, "What's her name?" Lately, I've seen
god in the most devilish people. Prime example,
my stepfather: a drug dealer who hands out honey-
baked hams & space heaters every Christmas.
Did you know not one black Jehovah's Witness
voted for the first, and undoubtedly last, African American
President of the United States, even though
word in the barbershop is that Jesus himself
seriously considered coming back to cast his ballot?
Maybe I'm wrong, but I refuse to get on my knees
and pray to a complete stranger. Besides, what if
the only thing you and another person have in common
is hair like wool? Sometimes I hear voices—Ella, Sarah, Billie, Nina.
Four women, who have each confirmed
I am not like jazz. I am swinging on the cusp
of blues. And yes, maybe all of this is reason enough
to make an appointment this week to see
a therapist, but one more day of vertigo
may be just what the doctor orders.

Haiku

Sometimes three lines be the only universe this poet can balance.

III.

The Enigma of Sin from the Perspective of a Former Jehovah's Witness Kid

i.

Every year the Memorial comes around
like a silver tray of unleavened bread,
wine—fragrant as a waft of Welch's grape juice.

I think *lord, I hope it hurries up and passes over me.*
praying no one, especially my father, appointed
usher, accidentally spills the blood of Jesus.

ii.

Each time the vein-red fluid
is transferred from one adult
hand to another, I consider the risks.

Study the smudge-free goblet,
about the size of the plucked apple,
an apple like the one I heard lured Eve.

iii.

And who can blame the woman
for wanting to reach out her perfectly formed hand
and place her mouth on its bare skin

just as she had done with Adam, watching
from afar, like a mischievous boy
or perhaps a girl who just had to see

what would happen   if
her mucky little fingers came in contact with God's
glass slipper made to fit only those drafted
in that pious number—144, 000.

iv.

And who can blame the child seated
in her steel folding chair tampering
with formality asking all the "wrong" questions.

An answer darts from my mother
whose quick fire glance let me know—
I don't have a monkey's chance.

Nonetheless, I am curious and would like a second
opinion. Like my forefather, Adam, I watch
the serpent in me take hold of my hand.

On the count of three, we place it on
the stem of the wine glass to see if God
and only God would speak to me *directly*.

Growing Up JW

In a Jehovah's Witness household you will go to school and sit quietly in your seat while the rest of your classmates stand up like good little children to salute the American flag. During the month of February, you will decline Ms. Maxwell's home-baked cupcakes weighted with pink frosting, red sprinkles and heart-shaped cinnamon candies. Not because you are on a diet or diabetic, but because it is against your religion. The religion passed down to you like the underclothes on your back. Gently used toys from a cousin's play box. Your first grade teacher, who seems just as confused as you are, makes a reasonable inquiry—"*Eating cupcakes?*" as if interrogating Jehovah, himself. Sticking to the script, you correct her by saying, "No, eating cupcakes on *Valentine's Day.*" After shaking her head in what could only be utter disgust, she will bypass your desk, but not before handing your designated treat to Tommy Terrell all the while mumbling something about how it is a shame the way children get treated in *that* religion. The religion your parents belong to. The religion that has become yours by default. But what's a 'JW' kid to do? Besides create a scene every morning during the pledge of allegiance ensuring that you will be remembered as the lone pagan who stood out for refusing to stand up. Mid-recitation, you picture yourself being turned into a block of salt while glancing back to see if anyone else is out of formation, only to discover every heart is crossed except yours—naked as Adam and Eve. Despite the urge to succumb to worldly ritual, consequences are clear as the disappearance of Jonah. So when offered the part, you politely decline playing the Indian—or worse, the turkey— in the annual Thanksgiving production. Your classmates ask questions. But there are limited answers. Not to mention the "no Christmases allowed" policy is not a good selling point. But in a family of followers few members are interested in what you think. Understanding the End is near, you do yourself a favor & forget about dressing up as the *black* Michael Jackson for Halloween. Striking poses with Santa. Decorating eggs hard-boiled for the occasion. Soon the lines between perk & punishment become one big biblical blur. Like when you get pulled from school early on the day of the party blocking all hopes of Corey Brown slipping you a card that reads: "Will you be mine?" I imagine most children do not develop an obsession over signs of last days. Aside from Orphan Annie, few know anything about a *hard knock* life. I'm talking every Saturday morning, when most kids in my neighborhood were still lounging around in pajamas. Stuffing mouths with Cap'n Crunch by the spoonful between giggles triggered by the animated antics of one wily little rabbit. Not me. I was out walking door to door. Handing out pamphlets. Spreading the good news. While my foundry employed father clutched his leather briefcase & smiled. Promising complete strangers the gift of everlasting life & pristine weather.

Places I Have Seen God

in the parched throat of a mosquito
in a pillar of salt
in the manufactured gleam of an apple
through the eye of a dark & jealous cloud
in the evolution of a tumbleweed
in the sanctuary of spooning lovers
between the legs of my older sister in the delivery room
in the cupped hands of the homeless
in the slingshot of David
in the dead air of an absent father
in Thanksgiving turkeys lined up
in the naysayers of now & Noah's time
in the sleeping womb of another man's wife
in an aerial view of ruptured levees
in the soft black gums of Mother Earth
in the pink tongues of liars
in the fig leaf image of a naked male body
the sensuality of a burning bush
in the parting of a woman's red sea
through the seduction of talking animals
in serendipitous streaks of lightning
in the flicker of a coin upward-faced
in the snaking backward of time
in the coiled locks of my own existence
in a parade of rainbows after the Flood
in the *god don't like ugly* mantra
in atonement
in the Sodom & Gomorrah of adolescence
in the genuflection of a team of Kaepernickers
in the kinship between a stuttering Moses
& my father
the dimming of Light at the end of all tunnels
in unreported sightings of sandaled Black men last seen
walking on water

Eyewitness Account

after Gwendolyn Brooks

In the dream I swallow a hard-boiled egg with a slightly cracked shell. It is lodged in my throat and I am unable to scream for my mother. Only god knows I am in trouble. He is busy with another patron so I administer the Heimlich to myself. Instead of the egg, my unborn child slides from my throat. The yolk is a viscous yellow river streaming down my legs. The child without a tongue is screaming and crying. I am screaming and crying. And backing away from the thick eye lashed thing with a head full of hair that has already ruined my breakfast. *Abortions will not let you forget.* Shards of black snow fall outside my window. Reams of unisex baby names scroll down from the sky. A flock of featherless chicken in blood stained lab coats cross the road. When they get to the other side—one of them proceed to dust the scene for fingerprints. Naturally, I begin to wonder about the dirt underneath some men's fingernails—a slight fixation of mine. As is ruminating about whether or not the hands of god are really clean. Starting with those immaculate dealings with Mary. With women. Women, in particular, who have reason not to believe in miracles. You see, I, too, was sleeping, most likely snoring, when the oval specter entered my body.

Sphinx

in memory of Michael Jackson

How do you deface
a piece of art, a *culture?*
aim straight for the nose

Glass Slipper

There I was on a Norwegian cruise line when a man I had only seen once in a previous life smiled and waved in my direction as if he recognized me, too. It was the strangest coincidence, yet I returned the friendly gesture with equal warmth. We weren't lovers, though we came close to being more than friends. Problem was, his girlfriend had accompanied him on the same trip, which he was planning to unveil as a "pre-wedding honeymoon." At first, I wanted nothing to do with the affair. But something about floating on the whisked wind's ebb interested me. There I was, locking eyes with an angelic faced version of the devils my mother had warned me about. Like how they enter the room having nothing to hide—designer pumps fiercely positioned on the opposite side of his bad shoulder. The one he is occasionally seen massaging at the gala. When he gives the signal, she misses her cue, or simply refuses to board the train—despite the strobe lit seduction of a seventies oldie but goodie. And you think to yourself, *it is none of your business*, whatever the pinch. Needless to say, one woman's worn heel is another woman's glass slipper. It all begins with an innocent bump on the dance floor. The sharing of fruit with no seeds attached. The proverbial glance in the mirror reflecting an image you hold dear. That of you being *the good girl.* The one who would have never bitten the apple or tripped head first while running circles around the devil.

Where Do Broken Hearts Go

poem for Lady Day, Joplin, Winehouse, and "the Voice"

Ever heard the one about the famed singer
who either drowns in the limelight or the tub?

The one where Billie, Janis, Amy, or was it *Whitney*
got so clean once that on the day she resolved

to take her last & final hit—it really was the last,
final hit. Some records have a way of turning

Judas on you after you have been found birth canal
naked, face down in your hotel room surrounded

by bottles: unlabeled pills of prescription this
& that—alcohol being of least scandalous fodder.

By now, it is no secret: autopsies are for celebrities
who die for a living. And then there are those

whose hired hands are more than willing to work
overtime in the event of one's untimely collapse:

removing fingerprints left on powder smudged
razors, disheveled nightstands captured in tabloid

photos: blood-leaked to the public reenacting
a star's submerging moments to last seconds.

True story—sometimes Death sticks out its stiletto,
or lures your anorexic soul out onto a balcony

offering a new multimillion dollar contract equivalent
to a red carpet plunge off a pier. Other times,

it is simply slipped inside the open hand like keys
to the city or perhaps your next number one *hit*.

Consider This

poem for Shayla

when your own mother

does not believe you

does not want to believe   you

believe that was the reason

you never told anyone

after all this time   what he and he

and even one of her former boyfriends

did or *tried* to do to you—

look her deep in the eyes

to see if there is a light on

in the dark and lonely   basement

where perhaps   she too

had been   violated

by some trusted adult.

IV.

S. S.

Those who are looking for trouble will radio it in—

describe the Black man or child last seen
playing in the park with a toy pistol, roaming
the gated community wearing a dark hoodie *or was it a skull cap?*
firmly positioned on the clean shaven head
of the man, the one who hijacked the vehicle
with babies still strapped in their car seats
yelling for their mommy, the brunette beauty
pageant reject who they say fell for a knight
in corporate armor, the pin-striped playboy
who made it beyond clear he did not want
any children nor a woman he could not

take seriously: southern, white, and redneck too.

Never imagined the young divorcée would call his bluff.
Grant his unuttered wish. Eject from her womb
every trace of blood, diaper rash'd flesh, smudged
end tables, crayoned walls, random spills
of sippy cups. Sud-soaked images of giggly
little boys spitting bubbles, bobbing heads
of rubber duckies in shared bath water.

Unlike Michael and Alex, Tom asked
for it. Not returning her calls. No longer
scheduling time for midday quickies.

Susan Smith: former Honor Society member.

Union County local-turned-first-degree murderer
convicted of drowning her two sons in exchange
for a mere do over in the town where everybody
can place a finger on your senior class photo—freckles,
bucked teeth, bouffant hairdo, innocent smile.

The town where you can recall make & model
of the first car you ever made out in.
The keys you handed him that night
so he could do all the driving.

Take you places you had never been before.
His parking lot hot mouth circling
every block, his revved tongue
skidding dangerously across one
little white lie after another.

Full Moon Morning

I awaken to the sound of Stevie Wonder broadcasting
very superstitious, writings on the wall. Set out to make coffee

before noticing an army of ants must have wanted a cup, too.
Can only mean one thing—somewhere there is a black cat

or panther crossing an ominous path. On the television, a Hispanic
anchorwoman reports: the death of Trayvon Martin is still

under investigation. Awaiting further unrest, I pour myself a mug
of green tea instead of French Roast. Ever cautiously, take a sip.

My stomach becomes a grave reminder of Emmett Till,
Amadou Diallo, Christopher Wallace—all murdered.

All buried children of someone still expecting justice
to be served. Even the Black president knows the score.

Encountered the *Autobiography of Malcolm X* pre-Harvard.
Acknowledged the fact that if he had a son, he, too, might

have been hunted down by some blood-thirsty, werewolf
howling, *Twilight*-turned-vampire, extraterrestrial freak alien,

9 mm wielding *RoboCop* by-product of American culture
& although I am a poet, I do not possess the power to slay

invisible dragons or intercept the next child's pubescent
"wolf whistle" from ricocheting repeatable nightmares

into the universe, but I can at least pick up the phone
& dial the number to one of my favorite male cousins

in hopes that before the 13th ring he will answer—
saggin' jeans, dark hoodie, Swisher sweet smile still intact.

for colored boys who have considered suicide/
when the voice of tupac was not in arm's reach

"penitentiary"

taking belts
from black
men drops
them down
a notch or two
grade levels

"p. s. #112"

when remedial reading
between the ask cracks

is not enuf, when the tag
sticking out does not say

Hanes might be strange
fruit of the loom hang-

ing around looking
for trouble or either   rescue

"walls of respect"

if rainbows come in all shapes   & backdrops
where might a young T. H. U. G.
begin to look for his father other than
the mythical L. I. F. E. he has tattooed
across his steel bar chiseled torso

"all eyez on me"

a wiser than streetwise
young man once observed   a boy will
learn how to raise himself
in a hard-ankle'd garden
concreted with roses
blackly blossoming   just like him.

How to Kill a Cop With Kindness

First of all, please show some respect
for the law by speaking in plain non-colloquial
English. None of that "Aye, yo, what up,
officer, is there a problem?" nonsense.

Obviously, he pulled your black ass over didn't he? Keep it real.

Take two—"Hello officer, um . . . I was just
wondering . . . did I do something
to possibly get myself potentially placed
in a chokehold, today—Imjussayin?"

If he shoots you a look as if he thinks you might
be a "nigga wit an attitude," neo savage, "hulk"
or one-eyed "demon" with a death wish, *please, please,*
do not, I repeat DO NOT make any sudden moves.
Just throw your hands in the air & wave 'em like you just don't
want to be too far ahead of schedule for your own
funeral. Then with all the yassum boss plantation
bowed head samboisms you can muster—coon
operate with the law. (*trust me, it is not worth*

a second autopsy later) While he or she is running a check
on your information, pray the cop you are dealing with
is not a *total* asshole. Is someone who, perhaps, believes
in the lord. Not like Dylan Roof or Mother Teresa,
but, like Black people, a people who have always
demonstrated more humanity & civility than
this country has ever been able to withstand.

Last, but not least advisable, whatever you do
DON'T blame it on the make, model
or your own failure to signal a lane change.
Chances are you would have been
pulled over even if you had decided
to crawl to your destination that day.

Holding Court With a Supreme Uncle Thom

poem for Ol' Clarence

Truth is stranger than
fruit—*blacker* the berry
sweeter the pluck.

Positive Supports Academies

this is every single one of us
calling into the future & getting a dial tone   a broken swing
alongside a seesaw of motives   this is a yellow-taped playground

this is "Atlanta Child Murders" exhumed
this is beyond *Scared Straight* forty years later
taped live in front of an unplugged audience

this is a curved penal pipeline
leaking oil from the nation's womb   babies dying
faster than cells can be erected

this is corporate cock blocking of a different poke
this is the white sheet removed
exposing your friendly neighbor

this is Board of Education's plan B: lock-in
lock out, lock down—swallow the key
I know why the caged bird spits bars

this is the mayor holding a lit torch too
this a bird—no, a plane—no, the owl
in Baraka's poem watching somebody   blow up

the school building from the inside   *whooooo next?*
this is the cat (without the hat) had Kanye's
tongue drifting from the teleprompter   this is the *other* shoe

that dropped on our children   dropped from burning
Bushes, tarred memory, flying melon
seeds plunging into American soil

this is 'hell to pay' & other clichés
'big & black' & 'slick as oil'
this is Bigger Thomas, the sequel

this is "No Child Left Behind"
come back to haunt like a three-thumbed
fingerprint smeared on pexiglas.

53

a theoretical ebonistic philo/soul/logical breakdown

*Every black American is bilingual, all of us. We speak street vernacular
and we speak job interview.*
—Dave Chappelle

shoulda woulda
couldas
run in tha same circles

wit *gonnas*
who ain't never *finnah*
do nuthin' but cept'

continue ta pruhcrassinate
an blow hot air
out da side o' dey neck

so stop keepin' comp'ny
wit tha *maybes*
who thank they prolly might

an start 'sociatin'
wit da *sho nuffs*
who fuh ackshully *did*

Hot Buttered Grits

These poems had to be boiled in water. Opposite
of Minute Rice heat & serve quick cups.
Simmered next to Alabama greens. Big Mama's
fatback & brown beans. Aunt Effie's homemade
buttermilk biscuits. Miss Louise's cornmeal
dredged freshwater catfish. This is how we do it.

Women who do not play in the kitchen or mince
emotions as if they were garlic. A pinch of salt.
Idiom slow-cooked. Aroma thick with the scent
of finely chopped shallots sautéed in real butter.
So these recipes stay on his breath even when
he leaves one roof to go break bread under another.

> *Love'll make you do right, love'll make you do wrong,*
> *Make you come home early, make you stay out all night long*

And with the drop of a needle on a suddenly turned
table, the range-top porridge thickens. Some women
have no trouble swallowing back kisses that taste
less & less like where he says he's been when
he comes home *three o' clock in the morning* hungry
for the one thing he can't get no place else.

Home cooking is like poetry—an art and an omen.
While the coffee black steam from a fresh pot would've
served him right, Mary chose to make her point
by reaching for the nearest weapon she could find
leaving a smoldering record of a woman's love
& unhappiness scalded into his memory.

> *Love'll make you do right, love'll make you do wrong,*
> *Make you come home early, make you stay out all night long*

Words like 'I love you' are so final.
Entering the flesh like a bullet. Each syllable
clinging to the candle waxed sweat on
the small of one's back. Trajectory
unstoppable. Connotation impalpable.

I am a believer in all things holy as sin
like the gospel of tambourine & horn colliding,
the midnight siren of falsetto screaming
the lord's name in vain. Takes the soul
of Al Green to remind some folk—
black poems have to be boiled in water.
Hot-buttered grits that they are.

"In Love / Struggle / Pen"

for Sonia Sanchez

1

Black men can't you see
my heart is in your hands don't
clench your fists so tight

2

Katrina's Deluge

Katrina submerged
homes FEMA flooded spirits
tears break levees too

3

It is the poets
who make the square world go round
orbiting language

4

How come Bojangles'
earnings tap danced in little
Shirley Temple's shoes?

5

The *n-word* is just
another excuse to still
call you a nigga

6

Civil Rights Movement in 17 Syllables

That day Rosa got
on the bus *in transit* to
our liberation

7

Blk Arts in 17 Syllables

I wish rap would (*w*)rap
its lyrical mind around
the power of words

8

Million Man March set
the tone but what have you done
since you marched back *home?*

9

If our Black youth have
no 'culture'—whose fault is it
they've lost their *black* minds?

10

Wo/manifesto Haiku

*To the people, speak
the truth,* says Mari Evans.
Says Sonia—*write on!*

Hottentot Redux

I heard Hottentot had a lot of bang
for her *boogie* except there were no music videos
back then to mass exhibit an *ass*-tounding
back end. So bodacious, so profound named her
"Hottentot Venus" since then—world been spellbound
by the gluteus maximus   historical facts of us
baaadmamajama brickhouse throwbacks of us
next generation Hottentot sensations.
Daughters of the diaspora merited for we inherited
through our DNA the ancestral endowment
BET now puts on display. Black Exaggerations
Television, I say. While you say—"Go head, baby
shake that money maker!" But I remember
when the European used to und(rape) her.
I remember when a British surgeon used
to take her on exhibitions around the globe
place her on stage then make her disrobe
so all the world could behold his *money maker*
& much like the British doctor who first pop-locked
& dropped her down from her regal status—today's mass media
simply continues the practice of reducing
African anatomy to sideshow freak.
It's in the jeans, I guess. Tailor made to parade
the Black female physique. Captivating
audiences with the curvaceously unique
badonkadonk Booty-licious© a.k.a. BabyPhat™.
It's in the jeans, I Guess™. After all,
wasn't it Eve who learned to deceive
Adam with the Apple Bottoms™.
It's definitely in the jeans.

Now may I direct your attention
from form-fitting low-sitting denim jeans
to form-fitting uplifting historical genes
where she be descendant of majestic
African queens. Ages before rap MC's
popped bottles, Black women were deemed *America's Next...*
correction, Tyra—first—*Top Models*.
Shapers of civilization. Epitome
of honor. Ungraspable beauty.

Vanity Fair has to be unfair it's their *Cosmopolitan*
duty to reject & dissect 21st century Hottentots.
Funny how what goes around comes
back around Botox now other women gots—voluptuous
lips, hips, breasts & thighs while Black women
got radio shock jocks & Hip Hop lyrics
that vandalize. So when Imus called us "nappy headed hoes,"
some said he had a point as we watched him point
to our videos where one can sit for hours & hours
& watch roles upon roles of present day minstrel footage
documenting: so-called 'nappy headed hoes' the now glorified
western images of Black beauty   Black culture
Black spectacle in the making   so we see, baby
got back & backwardness for the taking. Modern
day minstrel footage on the tube gyrating. Rap
artists in black face as village griots narrating
our story, chronicling our times. Recording
our so-called 'progress' for the supply &
demand of human freak show fetish
from "Hottentot" to hot to trot
from exhibitions to hip hop auditions
from carnival attraction to video vixen
no more "oddity" now "hot" commodity
droppin' it, poppin' it, lockin' it—phenomenal
women's bodies be once more on the world stage
shaking what our mamas gave us. 'Low & behold'
What now enslaves us? as cameras zoom in to gawk
once again at the outs & ends of us from lopsided
angle much like the caricatured profile of our beloved sister
Sarah Baartman who at this historical juncture
must be turning over in her South African grave
from witnessing myriad women of color forget
to remember why perhaps we should *not*
drop it like its Hottentot.

V.

A 'Slave' By Any Other Name or Fame

> *"I was the conductor of the Underground Railroad for eight years, and I can say what most conductors can't say —I never ran my train off the track and I never lost a passenger."*
> —Harriet Tubman at a suffrage convention, NY, 1896

1. Sticks & Stones

Nigger—a southern sensory overload. A Cajun spice. A blackened
cross. A pungently aromatic experience sparking memory loss
in some. Memory recall in others. Ask my father if he answers
to the phrase, *boy*. With the quickness, he will make it plain
even if his tongue should stumble over a string of lowercase
g's—his mama named him *Jimmie*.

2. Water Millions

Inside the summer sweet & fleshy mouth where the roof is as pink
as tall tales are white: Paul Bunyan. Kris Kringle. Johnny Appleseed.
I can recall my own father planting a story in my head about the time
he almost met the fate of Emmett Till while visiting cousins
down south where a silver-bearded store clerk leaned over
the counter to ask, *What kinda gumball you say you want, boy?*
My dad, more accustomed to northern hospitality
mistakenly looked him in the eye then replied, *huh?*

3. A Long-Haired Legacy of Susan Smiths

You don't know what you don't know until
all you know is that a kid your age
had not only lost his tongue but also an eye
for pursing his big city lips at a white woman.
From that moon forward, it is not only the sound
of whistling wind that can make your watery
soul quiver. It is the thought of one of them
opening their beauty pageant mouths
at any given slip of the hand or wheel
to then point the finger at you.

4. On Becoming A Self-Made Man

Growing up in Greenwood, my daddy lived it. Indianassippi still
breathes it. From root words to root causes. The stretching of industrial
arms & legs into Midwest territory. A heartland bleeding profusely.
A circular city more squared than not. Known for its bi-colored
cornfields. Burgeoning rows of clotheslines dangling crisp white sheets.
At the 'crossroads' of America, a young man stands firm at age 20.
Chooses the name Lee Iacocca over Horton & Sons Trucking.

5. Carter G. Woodson: Black History Week

Wheels are for re-inventing not nomenclatures—coon,
Mantan, Stepin Fetchit, Jigga. Games like Cowboys
& Indians: American pastimes like polaroids & picnics
souvenir'd into postcards parading the peculiar institution
of patriotism. Add to this—slave auction re-enactments
in public schools like McFarland Elementary where I
witnessed a white female teacher introduce to a classroom
of self-proclaimed Black African "booty scratchers"
the *Life and Times of Frederick Douglass* who, by the way,
she referred to as "the most famous *slave* ever."

6. Black History Month

I wish I were lying about the problems our children face
not knowing their history. Not reading between the beats
& hooks. Lyrical nooks. Industry crannies. The old versus
new lingua franca. But, ain't nothing friggidy fresh under
the sun, my nigga (formerly nigg-*er* per Paula Deen when
not stuffing her jaws with post-antebellum hog maws,
southern fried chicken, candied yams & collard greens) *nah mean?*

7. Malcolm X: The Ballad or the Bullet

Not since Twain has the 'n-word' gained
so much class & cultural capital   *cha-ching!*
Not since Hova & Yeezy have we given
an entire generation our historical
backwash & material blessings.

How come we got 99 problems but gettin' jiggy with a confederate flag ain't one?

All I know is Harriet Tubman
would kill for an opportunity
to come back here to find
this many "New Slaves"
seemingly uncertain
about which way is Up.

Post-Racial American House Negro Or Is It the Pot Calling the Kettle Black?

What a Thom

ass. Wishing upon

a falling star

for affirmative action

to go out like

a deferred ambition.

He who specializes

in nightmares

& other wake-up calls: some knee—

grows want to keep

us as *boxed*-in

as Aunt Jemima

& Uncle Ben.

All Jokes Aside

I saw the William Shatner roast, and the Pamela Anderson roast, and it whuddn't all about them being white. But on Flavor Flav shit, every other word was 'Flav is a crispedy, crackally, crunchedy, coon . . . He's a black, sizzly, crunchedy, crackelly, coon. Flav is a big black crispy, crackally, crunchedy coon' all through the fuckin' script.
—Comedian Katt Williams, Pearl Concert Theatre, 2007

1. "Burn Hollywood Burn"

Paying tribute to Flavor Flav,
the packed house of Hollywood & Hip-Hop celebrities
nearly died laughing, nearly cried themselves
a river of blood, sweat & jeers
nearly broke a barbecued rib.

2. "It Takes a Nation of Millions"

After the drumroll, there was a roar of southern
fried chuckles careening through a crisp coon
cacophony *of hambone, hambone, have you heard*
the one about your mama jokes. Diamond studded
hand claps in syncopation with silver-spooned
knee slaps—all under the guise of good "clean"
entertainment. Yet I failed to see the humor
in off-colored "colored" jokes ricocheting off the shackles
of a 21st century class act fool wearing gold
teeth, a Viking helmet, Kool-Aid purple suit
& "a big ass clock with the wrong g—damn time on it,"
sitting in a high-backed chair cracking up
& cracked out just-a-laughin' & a-laughin'
counter-clockwise circles around himself
because being reduced to a "burnt piece of toast"
at the celebrity roast on national television
is almost as comical as being a black male
& surviving the odds to go on to become
the quintessential hype man for Public Enemy, *first*—Tinseltown next.

Now, that's some funny shit.

66

As is falling to your ashy knees in front
of millions while sucking down racist insults
through a plastic straw instead of a glass pipe.
Especially, to a predominantly white audience
who remembers your black ass when   *You gotta fight the powers that be!*

3. "Yo! Bum Rush the Show"

You mean to tell me—even with an African American
president we are still the butts of the "crunchedy" "crackally"
jokes?   *Holy smoke*! Speaking of joke, Flavor Flav, man,
you so Black. You soooooooooooooooooo black,
that when you shut your eyes to go to sleep at night,
I bet you think you in a closed coffin. *Imjussayin'*
'cuz when you can no longer feel the pulse of your people
disowning your J. J. Evans-jive-thug-Urkel-yassah-boss
plantation relapse watermelon-greased-neo Sambo
Chicken George swag. Magical negro reincarnated
in poster B-Boy stance. New millennium black face
in "black face" caricature of your black face   *real talk*

when you fail to notice long memory'd ones collectively
throwing out your Hip Hop street cred along with Wednesday's trash
brotha, you might as well be dead 'cuz all of America mocks
the once politically-informed-mascot-turned-minstrel-reality
tv star   *That's right, I said all of America* ridicules your cultural
back slide into self-parody. Mantan Moreland burlesquepopculture
clownism at its worst & ugliest. In all honesty Stepin Fetchit,
himself, would probably find your stage act laughable too.
Or else, outright heartbreaking. Unlike him you stumbled
upon an already paved platform. Still chose to shuck & shuffle
for the silver coin. Or in your case, for the "flavor" of love.

4. *Yeah booooooooyyyeeeee!*

So for the white male comedian who unabashedly
posed the question, "How do we roast *charcoal?*"
in reference to the guest of honor's cooked
to a crisp career overshadowing the room,
on live television where the packed house
of Hollywood & Hip Hop celebrities
nearly died laughing, nearly cried themselves
a river of blood, sweat & jeers.

Ay, yo! I got a line even more show stoppin'
than that one—How do you look at yourself
in the mirror, these days knowing 9-1-1
is no longer the joke in your town (*drumroll please*)————you are.

"What the Angels Eat"

Just when you thought he wasn't Black enough, Obama
faced the country in century old font across national headlines
& uttered the unthinkable——Trayvon could have been *my* son.

His infamous unsolicited "un-presidential" opinion
dropped the mic. Soiled the Whitehouse lawn leaving
a star spangled splotch on our immutable memory

of Emmett Till. James Chaney. Fred Hampton.
Jordan Davis. Amadou Diallo. Tamir Rice.
Laquan McDonald. All demonized before and *after* death.

This is just to say, one of them was reaching for his wallet.
Another, asleep in bed. Danger lurks in all roots & rinds.
But, what we have here is a special kind of berry grown

worldwide. Originated in Africa. Wild as it may seem,
has become known as the "official state vegetable" of Oklahoma.
Leaving one to surmise that all seeds not swallowed land

in somebody else's backyard. Become embedded in the margins
of who we are. Revamping the topography. Seeds unspittable
as history. Concreted in rural imagery like spokes of a red

wheelbarrow. Glazed with a single-mother's tears. A summer
staple wedged in the narrative like cornrows: hoodies: Pac.
So much depends upon whether or not all lives matter:

screenshots of America in the Sixties take us back to sit-ins,
fire hoses, torched churches: 'No Coloreds Allowed' signage.
'Whites only' memorabilia seldom emerges in the conversation.

Naturally, when the mixed race POTUS pins the tail on the mule
she kicks. Oh, what peculiar institutions we thread through the eye
one needle at a time: a widened mouth to fit the juicy description.

Teeth tall as tales of porch monkeys peeling jungle banana.
Yet, many a folk still decline to partake of this summer solstice
treat, as if my man Twain never dabbed his wiry 'stache

& huckleberry stained chin before publicly confessing
to the world that to taste a watermelon
is to know *what the angels eat.*

Microphone Check

While judging a local "youth
poetry and rap talent contest" . . .

   I saw the future of Hip Hop
    bleeding profusely from the corner
of its young black inventive mouth

   I saw the future of Hip Hop
    with a platinum bullet
lodged in its brilliant throat

   gangsta limpin' toward
    the edge of the stage
gasping for air *dying*
to be taken seriously

   through a Midwest lens.

Keeping It Indy 500

i.

I could chant *f--k tha police* but then what?
Join others at the Circle Centre Mall, downtown
Indianapolis buying fleece hoodies, Skittles.
Bottles of Arizona iced tea, yet who in Florida
is watching me stand my ground in a dimly lit Naptown
where our most popular spectator sport has a checkered
past, too. How come we keep going around in circles?
Same goals, different decade, same horror
film involving real life terminators fresh out
of the academy. Badged bullies who protect
and serve the only lives that seem to matter.

ii.

When our own Michael was murdered—16 years young,
while sitting in the backseat of a police cruiser. Hands
cuffed behind his back. We were told he must have hidden
"the gun" inside his sneakers *after* two cops at the scene
had already frisked the teenager. Unlike Watts (Newark,
Chicago, Detroit …) we took to the streets with community caution
Black souls in synchronization: Selma to Montgomery action
because *we shall overcome* (or was it because we thought we had).

iii.

We wore the only color we could find in our closets—collective Black
outrage. Sometimes we want answers when we already have them.
If a 22 year-old immigrant from Guinea can be gunned down
by NYPD while standing in the doorway of his apartment
building 'cooperating' with law enforcement, what you think
an American Black male got coming who insists on walking
in the middle of the street, in the middle of the day in his own
neighborhood, strutting fearlessly alongside one of his boys?
Both young men—Jordan heirs, shootin' hoops, smashin'
backs of rims confident in their unstoppable existence.

iv.

Young males who had not yet learned the line
between aggression and resistance. Wearin'
the only color they could find. Representin'
the only music aligned with their Struggle.
Capitalizin' on the only American Dream
they have ever been sold. A Black president.
A Hip Hop culture. A mouth full of *unmined gold.*

Cops 2.0

Cops

the show that don't show
the blows *real* cops throw

Cops

Yes observant children—tell-a-vision
cops have to wear a little makeup
in front of the camera to cover
their LA riot *blemishes*

Cops

Gotta quick-cut to commercials
for those scenes that can't be seen

Cops

Celebrating season 30
due to its winning formula
with seasons 1 through 29
that went a little something like this...

Out of shape white cop
meets *suspect* nigger who is seen
fleeing the scene
with OJ Simpson nerve
white cop stumbles
trying to cut sharp corners
in slum housing
can't clear fence
must call for back up to help
chase down *perp*
back up arrives in full force yet, is no match
for athletic Kunta . . . simply *"following police procedure"*
cops unleash "Charlie the K—K—Kanine"
finally, *suspect* nigger is NABBED! JABBED!
then APPREHENDED!
with savage fists tightly cuffed suspect is clearly SUBDUED

suspect is clearly SUBDUED
yet, simply *"following police procedure"*
brotha is *still* slammed
on the hard concrete
while television cameras *zoooooom*
in on the criminal hue
of his sweat drenched skin
so TV viewers can get a good glimpse
of the scuff marks framing
the face of Black & Brown America

Cops

Bad boys, Bad boys whatcha gonna do?
Whatcha gonna do when they come for you?

When they come for you with no lights! or camera!
to film Rodney King Amadou Diallo Sean Bell action!

Bad boys, Bad boys whatcha gonna do?
Whatcha gonna do when they come for yooooouuu?

When they come for you with no lights! or camera!
to film Michael Taylor Nathaniel Jones Abner Louima action!

Cops

> *Oscar Grant III*
> *Philando Castile*
> *Laquan McDonald*
> *Sandra Bland*
> *Charleena Lyles*
> *Aiyana Mo'Nay Stanley-Jones*
> *Freddie Gray*
> *Walter Scott*
> *Eric Garner*
> *Manual Angel Diaz*
> *Antonio Zambrano-Montes*
> *Aaron Bailey*
> ....
> ....
> ....
> ....
> ....

Indiana Avenue: Jazz-ku for Wes

Wes Montgomery
balanced his scales on the edge
of a blueblack thumb.

Black rivers flow up
ward their magnificence |fret|
ting the dams ahead.

Man, sometimes you got
to nudge the notes, only way
them blue ones gon' budge.

How can you not *redefine*
the only instrument you have?

"Straight No Chaser"

They have taken no
thing that was ours to begin
with including *blues*.

Bursting Bubbles

Bible tells us it is in our DNA to desire to bite off
more than we can stomach. We spit seeds east, west, north,

south and Neverland. A born king moonwalks across
a pool of sweat on the dance floor. Furnace burnt feet,

jheri curled hair like wool. Be careful what you pray for,
the crown, cleft chin, never-ending childhood, a new

Dr. Feel Good. Another hit. Your face chiseled into the Rock
& Roll Hall of Fame because *This is It* according to biological

countdown. In the aftermath, some *Smooth Criminal* will leave
you holding the syringe. Breaking news—another kid

has come forward to describe the can of Coke, M & M size
mole. Pointing fingers that glowed in the dark like E.T., grew

like Pinocchio underneath a shared blanket. Cover yourself
always. Some people get close because they want to see you

without the mask, nose, amusement park. Throne.
Should have asked Diana Ross or Elizabeth Taylor

about the perils of being obsessed with Hollywood extras:
penciled-in beauty marks, tattooed hairline, wigs, infamous

courtroom goatee. A vinyl portrait of a real life permanent
Thriller. Looking back, what are the odds—that the man

in the mirror only wanted children so he could
have someone besides a *monkey* on his back.

Hip Hop 'Lyrics of Lowly Life'

after Paul Laurence Dunbar

We wear the masc/u/linity that grins and lies,
It huffs and puffs and rides or dies,—
This burnt cork we apply backstage;
'with torn and bleeding hearts' we rage,
And tongues cock'd guns be aimed at black wombs.

Why must street griots conjure death,
through sixteen bars of brilliant breath?
Platinum grills bejewel us, while
   We wear the mask.

We bling, but O' bright youth, do look
Now strange fruit swing on hip hop hook.
We twerk, but ah the noose is taut
Around the necks of bling'd souls bought
But take heed while keeping it real,
   We be *illin'!*

word is bond (don'tshootthemessenger)

whazzup hip hop

on the flip flop

w/ your guns glock'd

& your head rock'd

ego on lock

w/your nuts cock'd

in position

on a mission

heading nowhere

nowhere so *fast*

i have to ask

are you aware

handsintheair

likeyoujuss*don't* care

that inside there

is a genius

is a genius

is a *genius*.

Tankas for MJ

after Patricia Smith

In this house, there will be blood on the dance floor until you get it right.

I am the boy browned
underneath stage lights hot &
funky like the moves
the "Godfather" owned—the *splits*
will part the soul black & white.

> In the beginning
> there was Gary & the blues
> of steel mills grinding
> mimicking a hunger in
> Joe's gut naming each child—*star.*

Joe passed down the gift
of discipline to his sons.
Soon, it would become
a household joke—what is Joe's
favorite MJ song? *Beat It.*

> Joe's home videos
> capture only the hard work
> not the discipline
> whipping the child prodigy
> into shape *warping* the soul.

There is no such thing
as the white Michael Jackson;
Black Michael is it.
Certainly, one might argue—
a *blue* Michael existed.

44th Presidential Haiku Memorabilia (rare collector's items)

Red, White, & Blue

How patriotic
is the swinging of 'red' states
making 'whites' go 'blue'?

2008 Election

Red states turned blue in
the blink of an Iowa
must be—black magic.

Wishful Thinking

Barack Obama
our president forty-four
acres & a mule.

Hood-ku

The Black president
speaks in code to the people
If I had a son—

The Day She: Mari Evans: Poet: Sisterfriend: Transitioned

i.

Today I got the news but it wasn't from Facebook.
An old friend had the decency to pick up the phone
& gently deliver the word so that I would receive it
in the most tranquil state possible—pulled over
on the side of the road, blinkers flashing.

Only respectable way to inhale death
when the person you've lost was close as a relative,
one who has never ever touched you sideways
or in between dank, dark slits of floorboards.
No dimly lit basements between us.

ii.

Her rare hand on hand touch, hard to earn smile
was a canvas of black suede holding a constellation
of *Nightstars*. A sacred hardback first edition
you never bothered to get signed
because she lived less than three minutes,
eight blocks & exactly fifty-two seconds away.
Because as long as Black poems exist
there would always be another next time.

iii.

Because despite her prolific though peripheral
celebrity, she was my friend, first and foremost,
which is to say, she was more than publications, Grammy Award
nominations, musical compositions, stage plays,
local "Black History month" cover stories.

More than distinguished guest speaker
in standing room only auditoriums
across college campuses but more so

82

because I had seen this phenomenal woman
rise *tall as a cypress* to bury one son
& then gravely another.
Take to her bedroom & keep writing.

iv.

As a spectator in box seats, I watched
the brevity of her verse *stay the course*
with political poems, community forums, paeans
to libraries, archived footage chronicling
the theatre of Black Experience.
Marveled at the uncompromised
fervor of a career-long "rebel"
one whose signature Black beauty
is internationally stamped on Ugandan postage.

Had a firsthand eyewitness account
that couldn't be bought or sold. Held in dangerous proximity
the secret to the truth of who we are.
Took inventory of her African walled home.
Arsenal of heritage and literary blueprint.
Wonderstruck that it was *this* woman
who had penned manifesto of all manifestoes
speaking BLACK ONENESS into flame
all from a presumed Naptown.

v.

Mari, our inimitable Midwest writer.
Call her anything but "Hoosier" poet.
Never played a note out of key or climate.
Walked around stupid like mud puddles. Pulled coat tails
of bustling young writers in her midst
with the eloquence of first-rate example.

One late evening, after working in the Blue room,
I cast my eyes on her sitting at the piano
(or was it the typewriter) making music
it seemed—for my ears only.

vi.

I was emerald green in those early years.
She was the color of clear black asphalt in the rain
when the streetlights go off or pitch blue blackness
permeating the vision of artists stumbling into walls
feeling their way around the slippery soul dark question
of themselves. She was (B)lack as universal language
can get. Bolder than urban idiom drawing lines
in white quicksand. Plainer than prose when
the singular motive for picking up a pen
is to unmask the messenger disguised
in the bling of doublespeak & moonwalk.

vii.

From her bedroom window, she could see it all—her people
coming, going toward & away from themselves.
Her typewriter had many miles.
Her rifle, I never asked.
It too sat by the bed as did a second library
of literature focused on American enslavement.

Spare them the fantasy. Fantasy enslaves.
My least favorite genre. Besides,
some Indianapolis neighborhoods
do not afford poets of deep color
the luxury to move about the landscape
disengaged from reality.

viii.

Framed to the walls of her chocolate-trimmed
three-story home are three oval-shaped
photographs: 1 aunt (dead), 1 grandmother (dead too)
1 (undeniable) father: stoic as a staircase.

They have met me at the door on many occasions.
Looked on as I heartily consumed hot plates
of this or that. Her quaint kitchen is where I
would experience stovetop coffee (for the first time).
Eat rhubarb in a "civilized" manner. Receive

cooking lessons on how to prepare spinach
artichoke dip & finely shredded coleslaw from scratch.
Slow sip everything from red wine
to Country Time lemonade heated
in a cautiously operated microwave. Often
downed my meals in uncomfortable silence—articulating
little as possible knowing I didn't know
half of what I thought I knew.

ix.

I was red, black & Generation X "green"
around the edges. She was the color of wisdom silvered
on the brow of foremother's learned
watchfulness. Her mural-esque stature
on Broadway preceded Mass Ave's
unveiling of the Indiana poet
whose unconquerable Vision. Love. Magnitude.
Stood 30 feet tall in real life.

Her perfectly plotted afro alone
would convict you if you were not
who you said you were at all times.

x.

Ms. Evans, a woman of her soft spoken words
didn't suffer idiots well, black ones, especially.

Rock star poets took note
of the *Dark & Splendid Mass*
of serious melody—lips full   hair, tightly coiled
& winced at the motion
the inescapable call & response:

Who
can be born black
and not
sing
the wonder of it
the joy
the challenge …

Home

is where the wheat is

      the sweet is of yellow corn

the vastness of virile plains

plunge & plow of tractors grinding

through thick soil: glacial sands, gravel, clay

producing fertile rows of fragrant harvest

signature as a Midwest skyline.

Home

is where the stretch of long road

smiles & smiles for emerald miles

where an abundance of local crops

choir crisp hymns in the rustic breeze   gently chant

praises of *cha-ching*   spit tufts of dirt

in the wind all eyes & ears pointing

toward the trough of bastard children

threatening to change the landscape

validating the question—*Hoosier* Daddy?

Yes, home of the jokes

that aren't funny   like Indiana*noplace.*

Like a baseball league of Negro

men labeled *Indianapolis Clowns.*

Like a reservation of sacred mounds

of charred Redskins belonging to Natives & Chiefs

whose roots be thicker than indigenous

lines drawn between wigwams & tepees.

Buried narratives idiomatic as *Indian-ah.*

Home

is where we have yet to reap all that has been sown

in the scalps of ancient memory

& on tongues of sun-dried bodies

dangling from blood-smudged photos

polaroiding klansmen, women

& owl-eyed offspring

learning *the ropes.*

Home

is where cross the tracks my parents

were educating *me* about ropes.

Today, I travel light when roaming

these historic parts of my beloved state   like Martinsville

where a Black female student en route to IU

can still stand face to face with sundown

signs: warning shots alerting my kind

that *I's gon be need'n to hightail it, after dark*

making Indiana

home of the "good lookin out" incentives.

Home of an ongoing campaign

to promote "reading" among minority youth

& home of the introduction on how to decipher

20th century American "sign" language,

but I have since learned how to burrow through

blurred perimeters   small-minded geography

where luminous night star & crossroads burn

clear. Tracking footprints of refugee

sharecroppers has landed me *here*

where I, too, have decided to plant my feet

in the heart of the capital's sky-scraping potential

so when one of my girlfriends living in D.C.

asks why I continue to relate to "such a conservative

state like Indiana" as *Home*

I simply tell her—border for border

it is the only place I trust.

Afterword

With her first collection of poems, *Quick Fire*, Allyson Horton takes us on a journey of personal and political revelations derived from her deep discerning of African American life and culture. *Quick Fire* opens with a celebration of African American women's persistent strength. From there, Horton invites us into her Indiana, Jehovah's Witness childhood, improvising on the theme of the Great Migration in the story of her own foreparents' unleashing themselves from the daily hardships and humiliations of Mississippi sharecropping. Inheriting "the struggle of an uprooted people," she rises as "Blackwoman poet" from the seeds they planted in "Indiana's wheat and wonder, corn and capitalism, possibility and surprise." No sphere of contemporary experience – personal or collective – escapes Horton's examination, including the rampant police murders of African Americans, the failed education policies affecting African American children, the degradation of African men and women in American popular culture, and the blues, loneliness and feistiness of betrayed women. Horton's grasp of such concerns radiates through profoundly moving, exquisitely crafted verse, reflecting her intense longing for justice. Her artistic brilliance shines in powerful masterpieces like her homage to Mari Evans – a wellspring of admiration and love, her protest against police violence in "Cops 2.0," and her ingenious updating of Paul Laurence Dunbar's "We Wear the Mask." Keen imagery carries us right to the heart of the feelings evoked – and sometimes there are sharp *signifyin'* blows to deserving clowns. The poet's diverse styles and tones switch like quick fire to convey humor, sarcasm, irony, or outrage, or to delight us with a touch of something earth-toned, rich and sweet that belongs to Black folk only, expressed tenderly in Southern Black speech rhythms and idiom. There is no "slipshoddiness [her term] of language" here: The poet is in perfect, sophisticated command. The reader regrets when the journey ends. We know that we will look forward to each new collection from this poet for years to come.

Gloria House, Ph.D.
Senior Editor
Broadside Lotus Press
Detroit

Acknowledgements

Deepest thanks to all who helped make this collection possible, each in recognizably special ways:

First and foremost, my publisher, Third World Press Foundation Dr. Haki Madhubuti and staff: Rose Perkins, Antoine Lindsey, Denise Billups, Willowlyn Fox, Adorn Mitchell—immeasurable gratitude for all that you have done for me.

Endless gratitude to Eugene Redmond, Kelly Norman Ellis, Gloria House, jessica Care moore—your recognition of my work is truly appreciated.

Butler University MFA Creative Writing Program, where my voice was understood, nurtured and sustained within the creative sphere of the Butler community: Alessandra Lynch, Chris Forhan, Dana Roeser, Susan Neville, Mindy Dunn, Dan Barden and David Shumate. Special thanks to Susan Sutherlin, Ania Spyra, Geoffrey Sharpless PhD, Anne Minnich-Beck, Efroymson Diversity Center, Butler Black Student Union, Terri Jett PhD, fellow classmates, former students and numerous other relationships that have helped make this journey both memorable and meaningful.

My utmost thanks and deepest gratitude go to Andy Levy and Hilene Flanzbaum PhD—whose unwavering belief, vision, and encouragement opened endless creative avenues all of which, helped lay the groundwork for my first volume of poetry. Thank you for giving me the opportunity and so much more!

I'd like to also express thanks to Park Tudor School—especially the English Department (heartfelt gratitude extended to Laura Gellin for so generously sharing your time and talents—hallmarks of a true *Artisan*). Special appreciation to Shants Hart. To all my students—*I am deeply inspired by you*!

Much appreciation is extended to Indiana University-Bloomington, Delta Sigma Theta Sorority, Inc. (Gamma Nu-Chapter), Dr. James E. Mumford Angela Brown. Indiana University-Purdue University: warmest thanks to Karen Kovacik PhD, whose creative passion, deep care, counsel and enduring friendship has been central to my journey as a poet within the Indianapolis arts community and beyond. Special thanks to Jim Powell, Mitchell L. H. Douglas, Dr. Ronda C. Henry Anthony, Mel Wininger, Missy Dehn Kubitschek, PhD, and Susan Sutton, PhD.

I would also like to express my appreciation to the following who have each had a significant impact on my life and work leading up to this publication: *It's Showtime at the Apollo!* ("The Stars That Spangle in the Banner"), Madame Walker Theatre, Elyria Kemp PhD, Kafe' Kuumba, Mari Evans (1919-2017), Eunice Knight-Bowens (1944-2013): The Etheridge Knight Festival of the Arts, Tony Radford ("Meet the Artists"), Amin Alghani (Moroccan Tea Company), David Allee (The Jazz Kitchen), Rob Dixon and the Indy Jazz Fest Band—I am grateful to have been able to poet alongside such an amazing ensemble of musicians. Special recognition to Old Soul Entertainment, Asante Children's Theatre, Freetown Village, Center for Black Literature & Culture, Indiana Writers Center, *Soul Liberation Radio, Indianapolis Recorder, NUVO,* as well as the vibrant collective of poets, writers, artists & musicians who have richly contributed to Indy's thriving arts scene.

Additional community appreciation is extended to Dona Stokes-Lucas— thanks for your abiding sisterhood, support, vision and legacy of Black literature and cultural X-Pressions. Mijiza Yaa Soyini—epitome of poetry in *serious* motion. Vickie Daniel—thank you, dear sister, for your selfless wisdom and inspiration. Sis. Mashiriki Jywanza & Family, Bro. James Officer, Cynthia Wood, Unequa Ganodu, Corey Pettigrew, Leroy Robinson, JL Kato, Congressman André D. Carson (IN-7). Tracy Mishkin (for your inner radiance and invaluable friendship), Rachel Sahaidachny, Gerry Justice, Amzie Moore, Elizabeth Davis and Mary Bradley.

Further acknowledgement and thanks to the following community circles: InterUrban Writing Group, Indiana Haiku Group (IHG) and the GOGIN2 Book Club.

I would also like to express additional thanks to Sydnee Haley for lending your artistic eye and creative impulse to this project. To the rest of my family—the poems in this book have loved you since their inception.

Grateful acknowledgement is made to the editors of the following publications where these poems first appeared, often in earlier versions:

The Wabash Watershed: "understanding eve"
Not Like the Rest of Us: An Anthology of Contemporary Indiana Writers: "The Mirror and Map of Memory"
The Indianapolis Review: "Haiku," "Indiana Avenue: Jazz-ku for Wes," and "Charlie's Horn"
It Was Written: Hip-Hop Inspired by Poetry: "for colored boys who have considered suicide/when the voice of tupac was not in arm's reach"

Notes

"The Enigma of Sin: From the Perspectives of a Former Jehovah's Witness Kid": *Memorial* refers to the Jehovah's Witness annual ceremony in which only the "anointed" members are allowed to receive communion during the "Memorial Service" which takes place annually in observance of the death of Jesus. The special ceremony is held in buildings similar to churches called "Kingdom Halls"; oftentimes, no one in attendance receives communion. Followers of the faith believe there is a "fixed" number entering heaven's gates (144,000).

"Hot-Buttered Grits": On Oct. 18, 1974, R & B singer Al Green became the subject of much conversation when his girlfriend, Mary Woodson, heaved a pot of scalding grits at his back. According to some sources, Woodson then fled to a bedroom, where she allegedly shot and killed herself with the singer's registered .38-caliber pistol. The infamous "hot grits" incident is believed to be responsible for the soul singers sudden turn away from secular music to gospel.

"Keeping It 500": The name *Michael* refers to Michael Taylor who died in 1987 from a gunshot wound while in police custody. According to the Indianapolis Police Department, Taylor was "able to reach a handgun hidden in his sneaker and shoot himself." FBI investigators backed up the story of IPD and the two officers who were involved at the scene. However, a jury would later rule in favor of the Taylor family in a civil lawsuit.

"Hottentot Redux": *Sarah Baartman* refers to "The Hottentot Venus."

"S. S.": On Oct. 25, 1994, Susan Smith told sheriff's deputies that a black man carjacked her Mazda Protege. The mother of two later confessed to drowning her sons in John D. Long Lake.

"All Jokes Aside": All quotations are taken from Katt Williams' stand-up special, *It's Pimpin' Pimpin'* with the exception of the fourth quote, which is taken from Jewish comedian, Jeffrey Ross' participation in the *Comedy Central Roast of Flava Flav* (2007). Ross later remarked: "Aw, come on, in these sensitive times, I'm not gonna do racial humor. Besides, the fact that Flav is 'black' is like—the *fifth* thing that's wrong with him."

"A Slave by Any Other Name or Fame": *Up* alludes to Marcus Garvey's famous words: "Up you mighty race, accomplish what you will."